20-Minute
Whittling
Projects

Dedication

There are folks put on this earth who never shy away from offering help to others. This book is dedicated to one such person—woodcarver Thomas G. Perrin. I "met" Thomas Perrin on the *Woodcarving Illustrated* magazine forum (www.woodcarvingillustrated.com/forum) in 2007. He answered my woodcarving question and offered assistance, as he did for so many others. I never met Thomas in person, but talked to him on the telephone several times a week until his death on February 4, 2011.

Acquisition Editor: Mindy Kinsey
Cover Designer: Jason Deller
Layout Designer: Justin Speers
Technical Editor: Bob Duncan
Producing Editor: Carly Glasmyre
Photography: Scott Kriner and Lindsay Garner
Step-by-Step Photography: Keith Radick

ISBN 978-1-56523-867-1

To learn more about the other great books from Fox Chapel Publishing, or to find a retailer near you, call toll-free 800-457-9112 or visit us at *www.FoxChapelPublishing.com*.

We are always looking for talented authors. To submit an idea, please send a brief inquiry to acquisitions@foxchapelpublishing.com.

Printed in Singapore
Ninth printing

20-Minute

Whittling

Projects

Fun Things to Carve From Wood

TOM HINDES

FOX CHAPEL
PUBLISHING

A *Woodcarving Illustrated* Book
www.WoodCarvingIllustrated.com

Table of Contents

Introduction

I titled this book *20-Minute Whittling Projects* because the projects in this book are designed to be completed quickly and easily. In my experience, a lot of early whittling publications seemed to focus on traditional whimsies like the chain, ball-in-cage, chain-in-cage, etc. However, these seemingly simple projects actually took a lot of time to complete and often discouraged beginners. I wanted to make whittling accessible to anyone interested in woodcarving, so I designed projects that help beginners start whittling without having to spend a lot of time or money.

It is my hope that the 18 projects in this book will get you started and develop your skills as a whittler. Each project can be adapted to your skill level, as you can incorporate more or less detail depending on how comfortable you feel. I divided the projects into four categories: Basic, People, Animals, and Baby Animals. With everything from farmers to pumpkins to elephants, you're sure to find the perfect project for you.

Even if you're not a complete beginner, I advise you to check out the Getting Started section as well as the Appendix in the back. These two sections will teach you everything from picking the right knife to whittling safety. Then, try the Sampler project in the Basic category. This project will give you practice with the basic cuts used in whittling (see page 86 in the Appendix for more information on basic cuts) and set the foundation for the other projects in the book.

What is Whittling?

Whittling can be defined as carving wood with only a knife; whittlers don't use chisels, gouges, or power tools. When people think of whittling, they think of specific projects: pointed sticks, wood chains, and a ball-in-the-box. But when I think of whittling, I think of any carving that involves only a knife.

That being said, whittling obviously doesn't require a large investment in tools or wood. All you need is a good knife, a good piece of wood, and a decent strop to keep your knife edge sharp. I give suggestions on knives and wood to use in the Getting Started section (page 8). If you aren't sure how to sharpen a knife, check out the Basics of Sharpening section (page 88) in the Appendix.

Whittling is a great hobby you can take anywhere you go. While some pull out their cell phones when they're in a waiting room, I work on my latest project! This is why most of the projects in this book are small—I like to choose pieces that can fit in my pocket. I also enjoy doing projects that can be completed quickly. This is what makes whittling fun for beginners—they get immediate gratification.

My whittling often attracts attention from the people around me, especially children. Children are the best audience for whittling because they like small things and they don't require too much detail to figure out what the whittled piece is. However, even if everything you make is for children, your piece will need some distinguishing characteristics. For example, elephants always have large ears and a long trunk, which are easy for both children and adults to identify quickly. The projects in this book will show you what features to leave in and what to leave out when depicting a person, animal, or object, and hopefully will inspire you to design your own whittling projects!

Getting Started

What Makes a Good Whittling Knife?

One of my favorite things about whittling is that you can do it anywhere. This means the knife you use should be easily transportable. I always use a folding pocket knife; nothing beats the convenience of safely slipping a folded knife into your pocket.

Many manufacturers create folding knives for whittling (or carving) with blades that resemble classic carving knives. These specialty knives can get expensive. They are worth the money if you do a lot of whittling, but you don't need to buy a specialty knife to whittle.

Many carvers use a second pocketknife for everyday use, such as opening cardboard boxes, to avoid dulling the sharp pocketknife they use for whittling.

When selecting a pocketknife for whittling, keep the following factors in mind.

Carbon Steel Blade

Many pocketknife blades are made from stainless steel. Stainless steel holds an edge for a long time and doesn't corrode if you close the knife with a wet blade—both great qualities for pocketknives. But because stainless steel dulls slowly, it sharpens slowly as well. Most carving tools are made from high-carbon steel. Knives with high-carbon steel blades are more expensive than knives with stainless-steel blades, but they are easier to sharpen.

Many manufacturers are creating high-carbon stainless-steel blades, which combine the durability of stainless steel with the added benefits of carbon steel.

Blade Location

Some pocketknives have 10 to 20 blades and attachments. These knives are generally less comfortable to use for long periods of time, and the blades you want to carve with are seldom in the center of the handle. If the knife blade is not in the center of the handle, you lose leverage, which reduces your carving power and control. Instead, look for a knife with two or, at most, three blades, which should ensure the blades are conveniently placed.

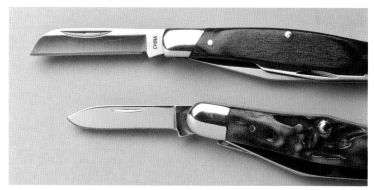

A sheepsfoot blade (top) is better suited for whittling than a drop-point blade (bottom).

Blade Shape

Look for a sheepsfoot blade—one where the tip of the knife is closely aligned with the main cutting edge, similar to a utility knife or standard bench knife. Many pocketknife blades have a drop-point shape, which centers the tip of the knife in the middle of the blade. The drop-point shape works well for general cutting purposes, but makes it difficult to carve small details. You can reshape a blade using sharpening stones and sandpaper, but the process is time consuming.

Locking Blades

A locking blade keeps the sharp knife from accidentally closing on your fingers, which is a good safety feature. However, as long as you are always aware a knife can close on your fingers, you should be safe, regardless of whether or not your knife features a locking blade.

Choosing the Right Knife for You

Selecting the ideal pocketknife for you is a matter of personal preference. The size of your grip compared with the size of the handle will greatly influence how comfortable the knife is to use over extended periods. The ideal knife for your friend may not be well-suited for you. Ask other whittlers for their opinions, but then hold and test several knives before making a purchase.

Basic Whittling Kit

As I've noted before, you don't need a whole lot to start whittling other than a knife and wood. However, it can be helpful to have a few extra tools handy. I suggest putting together a basic whittling kit so you have the essentials wherever you go.

My first suggestion is a carving glove. I always use a carving glove to protect the hand that is holding the wood. Proper hand positioning should keep the hand holding the wood out of harm's way; however, a carving glove is another good safety precaution.

Some projects, like my Sampler and the 15-Minute Santa, don't have a pattern and require you to draw simple detail lines. Keep a couple of pencils handy to sketch and draw detail lines on the wood. This is also great if you're on the go and you don't happen to have a pattern—you can just sketch one.

Finally, make sure to include a strop in your basic whittling kit. A strop maintains the cutting edge of your knife. I strop my blade before and after every whittling session; sometimes I even strop it during the whittling session.

Selecting the Wood

The main requirement in selecting wood for whittling is that the wood must be able to hold detail. To hold detail, it needs to have a tight wood grain and be knot-free. There are several species of wood that meet these criteria; however, for newer and less experienced whittlers, the wood should also be easy to whittle. In the United States, the species of wood that meets all of these criteria is basswood; in Europe, it is known as lime wood or linden wood. Basswood (linden) is readily available at modest prices. This does not mean that other types of wood cannot be whittled; it just means that generally, newer whittlers will have more success with basswood.

Preparing Wooden Blanks

Transferring a Pattern

Most whittling and carving patterns are in print form, as in this book. I suggest photocopying the pattern so you always have a master copy. You can also enlarge or reduce the pattern with a copier. When you're ready to transfer the pattern to the blank (wood), use graphite or carbon transfer paper. Place the pattern on the blank, slip a sheet of transfer paper between them, and use a few pieces of painter's tape to hold them in place. Trace the pattern with a red pen. Choose a light-colored transfer paper for basswood.

For multiple carvings of the same thing, many whittlers make a permanent pattern out of tag board, sheet plastic, or any other material that can be cut and easily traced onto the wood.

After you transfer the pattern, cut the perimeter with a band saw, scroll saw, or coping saw. Now you're ready to start whittling!

Projects

 There are four kinds of projects in this book: Basic, People, Animals, and Baby Animals.

The Basic projects include a Sampler, a Ball, a Whammy Diddle, and a Pumpkin Pin. These fun and easy projects will help you develop your whittling skills quickly. Then, you can apply those skills to create the projects in the following sections.

In the People section, there's the popular 5-Minute Wizard; the 15-Minute Santa; a Farmer that can be adapted to also make a leprechaun, an Uncle Sam, or a gnome; and a smaller Gnome. These whimsical figures are great for children or adults, and I encourage you to play with different finishing techniques to see how you can make the figures your own.

In the Animals section, there's a Dog, a Bear, a Gargoyle, a Horse, and a Fox. Explore whittling different breeds or kinds of each animal—for the dog, I show examples of a poodle, Scottish terrier, and boxer—and different sizes of each animal. I carved miniature horses to create earrings and made a large dog carving and a miniature dog carving to experiment with size. The best part of whittling is that there really are no rules for what you can create next.

Speaking of small carvings, the final section in this book is Baby Animals. It includes a Fawn, Piglet, Baby Fox, Bear Cub, and Baby Elephant. After you master the projects in this book, feel free to whittle other kinds of baby animals. If you're ready to branch out, I'd suggest staying away from exotic or obscure animals. Select an animal that children can recognize and relate to. Remember that the whittled baby animal may receive some rough play, so choose an animal that is a bit "chunky" and won't be too fragile when completed. When drawing or acquiring a pattern, try to use a side view or profile. When tracing and cutting out the baby animal blank, orient the pattern on the wood to eliminate weaknesses in the completed carving.

In years past, young girls were taught the basic stitches used in sewing. They made "samplers," which required them to repeat the basic sewing stitches over and over again. These samplers could be very simple practice pieces or more elaborate pieces with words and scenes. The thought behind this activity was: practice, practice, practice.

I created this whittling sampler so beginners could practice the basic cuts used in whittling: the stop cut, the push cut, and the paring cut. See Basic Cuts on page 86 of the Appendix for more information about them.

In this project, you will practice on each corner of the blank, as well as on one of the flat sides. On Corners 1 and 2, you'll make stop cuts and notches. This will prepare you for Corners 3 and 4, where you'll practice making noses and eyes. This will be particularly helpful for the projects in the People section of the book, but these skills can apply to any of the projects.

Materials & Tools

Materials:
- Basswood, ¾" (19mm) thick: 2" x 7" (51mm x 178mm)

Tools:
- Knife
- Ruler

Sampler: Making Stop Cuts

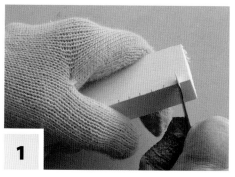

Make stop cuts on Corners 1 and 2.
Measure and mark the blank on two corners
at ¼" (6mm) intervals. Make a shallow stop
cut, about ⅛" (3mm) deep, at each mark.

Carve notches. Remove small angled chips
from each side of the stop cuts to make
evenly spaced notches. These are paring cuts
and push cuts.

Sampler: Carving Eyes and Noses

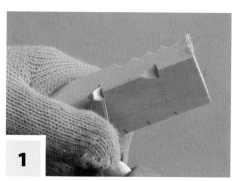

Carve the bottom of a nose. Measure
and mark Corners 3 and 4 at ¾" (19mm)
intervals. Make ³⁄₁₆" (5mm)-deep stop cuts at
each mark. Then, use a push cut to remove
a chip up to each stop cut. This will create
the bottom of a nose. Repeat at each of the
remaining stop cuts.

✎ Easier Stop Cuts

Now is a good time to start a
habit. When you're whittling
smaller projects, it is easier to
make stop cuts by moving the
wood into the blade rather than
by moving the blade into the
wood. You may not be able to
do this all the time, but practice
it whenever possible. Place the
blade on the measured mark,
hold it firm, and "rock" the piece
of wood into the blade to make
a stop cut.

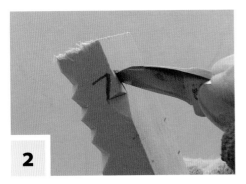

Carve a nose. Draw the nose and the tops of the eyes. Make stop cuts on either side of the nose by plunging the knife tip into the wood at the top of each side, and then rocking the knife blade down to the bottom of the nose as shown in the photo. Angle the blade to avoid undercutting the nose.

2

3

Carve the eye sockets. Make stop cuts at the top of each eye socket by plunging the knife tip into the wood where it intersects with the top of the nose, and then rocking the knife blade out as shown in the first photo. Then, using the knife tip, cut up to the stop cuts that define the sides of the nose and the tops of the eye sockets, and remove a chip from each side of the nose. The deep area where the cuts intersect is the eye socket. Make these cuts to form a nose and eye area at each of the remaining measured marks on this corner of the sampler.

4

5

Carve the eyes. On a flat side of the blank (between the corners), use the point of the blade to make two short, intersecting stop cuts. Then, remove the chip outlined by these two stop cuts with the point of the blade.

Add eyes to the eye sockets. Now that you feel comfortable, practice adding these "stop cut" eyes to the eye sockets on Corners 3 and 4.

Here's another project that will improve your skills—whittling a ball from a square piece of wood. Most whittling projects require rounding of some sort, and this project will make that easy.

Materials:
- Basswood, ¾" (19mm) thick: ¾" x 5" (19mm x 127mm)

Tools:
- Knife
- Ruler
- Pencil

Make stop cuts. Measure ¾" (19mm) from one end, and mark the measurement around the blank. Make stop cuts around the mark.

Carve the corners. Use push cuts and paring cuts to round the edges of the blank.

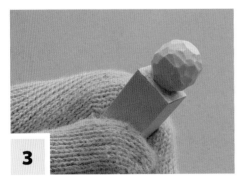

Finish the ball. Continue rounding the end of the blank with push cuts and paring cuts until the ¾" (19mm) square is completely round like a small marble. Then, cut it away from the blank and whittle another. The more you do, the easier it will become!

Whimmy Doddle, Gee Haw, Houey Stick—this simple little project is known by many names. It's easy to whittle and even more fun to play with. For those who don't know, a Whammy Diddle is a notched stick with a propeller on one end. When you rub the notched stick with another stick, holding your thumb and forefinger in certain positions against the notched stick, the propeller will spin in one direction. The real fun comes in when you make the propeller spin in a different direction using only your voice!

Materials & Tools

Materials:
- Basswood, ⅜" (10mm) thick: notched stick, ⅜" x 12" (10mm x 305mm)
- Basswood, ¼" (6mm) thick: propeller, ½" x 2½" (13mm x 64mm)
- Dowel, ³⁄₁₆" (5mm) diameter: rubbing stick, 8" (203mm) long
- Small nail, screw, or ball-end pin

Tools:
- Knife
- Ruler

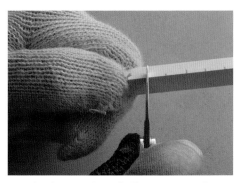

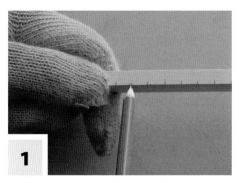

Make stop cuts. Mark the stick at ⅜" (10mm) intervals. Then, make a shallow stop cut about ⅛" (3mm) deep at each mark.

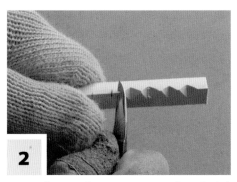

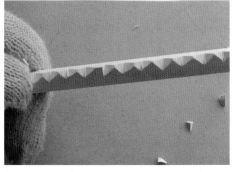

Carve the notches. Remove small angled chips from both sides of each stop cut to make evenly spaced notches.

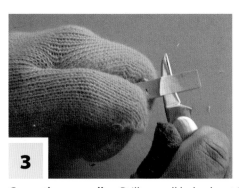

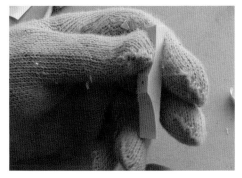

Carve the propeller. Drill a small hole about ⅛" (3mm) deep into the end of the notched stick for the propeller. Then, shave off strips of wood from the sides of the propeller with the knife.

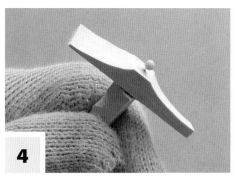

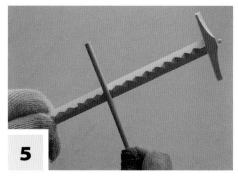

4 Attach the whittled propeller. Use a nail or pin to attach the propeller to the end of the notched stick. You may have to bend the pin slightly so the propeller spins freely.

5 Check the balance. Hold the notched stick in your hand to check if the propeller has the same weight on each side of the nail or pin. If the propeller is heavier on one side, remove a little bit of wood from that side, and recheck. Keep doing this until the propeller is balanced. After it is properly balanced, hold the notched stick in one hand and rub the other dowel up and down the notches. With a bit of practice, the propeller will start to spin!

How the Whammy Diddle Works

Hold the rubbing stick in your dominant hand with your forefinger extending over one side of the stick and your thumb on the opposite, lower side of the rubbing stick. There should be about a finger's width separation between your forefinger and thumb. Start rubbing the stick against the notches with your thumb touching the notched stick as you rub. The propeller will spin. Move your hand so your thumb is disengaged and your forefinger is against the notched stick as you rub. The propeller will change directions. Practice the movement until you can do it smoothly and coordinate it with some voice commands.

Pumpkin Pin

Seasonal pins are always fun to whittle and to give, and you can't think of Halloween without pumpkins! I chose to add a face to my Pumpkin Pin to make a jack-o-lantern, but you can also leave the pumpkin plain. There are an endless number of faces you can carve if you decide to make the pumpkin a jack-o-lantern. I chose to carve two friendly faces, but you can try your hand at carving scary, sad, or surprised faces.

Getting Started

Trace the pattern onto the blank, and cut around the perimeter with a band saw, scroll saw, or coping saw. Draw the detail lines onto the blank.

Materials & Tools

Materials:
- Basswood, ¼" (6mm) thick: 2" x 2" (51mm x 51mm)
- Acrylic paints (optional)
- Stain and wood conditioner (optional)
- Polyurethane

Tools:
- Saw: coping, band, or scroll
- Knife
- Paintbrushes (optional)

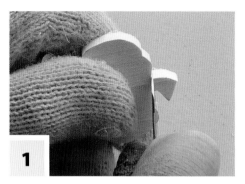

1

2

Carve the stem. Make a stop cut at the base of the stem. Thin the stem by carving down to the stop cut.

Shape the pumpkin. Round the pumpkin by removing small chips and slices from the outer edge. The goal is for the entire pumpkin to look round, so try to whittle away as many of the flat areas as you can.

3

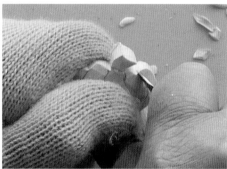

Carve the sections of the pumpkin. Redraw the sections of the pumpkin. Make shallow stop cuts where the sections of the pumpkin meet the edge. Remove a small chip down to the bottom of each stop cut. To make these stop cuts safely, start them at the outer edge of the blank and cut toward the center. Avoid running the knife blade over the edges of the blank.

✐ SAFETY TIP

When making a paring cut toward your thumb, always try to keep your thumb below the edge of the wood being cut.

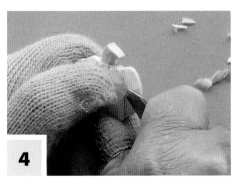

4

Define the sections. With the knife, make shallow stop cuts that define the pumpkin "sections," and then remove a thin angled slice of wood from each side of these stop cuts to separate the sections of the pumpkin. As in Step 3, avoid running the blade over the edge of the blank.

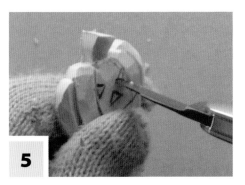

5

Carve the face. Using a pencil, lightly draw the eyes, nose, and mouth. You can carve a traditional jack-o-lantern face, as I did in this step-by-step, or something a little more nontraditional, like the jack-o-lantern featured on page 20. Make shallow stop cuts to define the mouth, nose, and eyes. Remove the chips that form the nose and eyes. Remove a thin slice of wood up to the stop cut that defines the mouth.

✐ Grain Direction

To establish the direction of the grain prior to starting a cut, start to remove a very thin chip or slice of wood to see if the blade digs in. If it does, you are carving against the grain; you should turn the piece and cut in the opposite direction.

6

Finish the pumpkin. It may be necessary to scrub the pumpkin with a stiff brush (such as a denture brush), warm water, and liquid detergent to remove pencil marks, dirt, or wood "fuzzies" at the bottom of cuts. If you scrub a piece, let it dry before applying a finish.

Front

Pumpkin Pin Pattern

Detail lines: --------

Finishing

There are several ways to finish the pumpkin: sand it smooth, leave the knife cuts visible in a flat-plane style, stain it, or paint it. Mix and match these finishing techniques or leave it unfinished. See the Finishing section in the Appendix (page 92) for more information. I painted the jack-o-lantern's stem green and brown, the body orange, and the eyes, nose, and mouth black. If the jack-o-lantern is to be a pin, glue a pin back onto the piece.

5-Minute Wizard

Materials & Tools

Materials:
- Basswood, ¾" (19mm) thick: ¾" x 4" (19mm x 102mm), cut in half to make two blanks
- Sandpaper
- Acrylic paint (optional)
- Stain and wood conditioner (optional)
- Polyurethane

Tools:
- Saws: table, band
- Ruler
- Knife
- Paintbrushes (optional)

When teaching woodcarving to beginners, I always wanted to create a project students could successfully finish in a single class. This 5-Minute Wizard is the perfect project for just that! I use this project for teaching basic carving skills and for demonstration purposes. I display carvings at gift shops, festivals, and art fairs; I've found that the actual act of carving will draw onlookers to my booth.

The 5-Minute Wizard is a simple project that can be given away to spectators. Children especially enjoy receiving a souvenir. I normally carve the wizards while I'm at the event, and then take them home to paint. I give the painted ones to onlookers while I carve a supply at the next event. It may take a bit longer to make your first few wizards, but once you have the steps down, you'll be completing them in about five minutes and can quickly carve a large supply. In addition to drawing attention at public events, they make wonderful little gifts for random acts of kindness. Leave one along with your tip at the local restaurant or give one to your favorite cashier. You can also attach a pin back or turn them into key chains.

Getting Started

As you prepare to whittle this wizard, read the entire step-by-step sequence before beginning.

The wizard is carved on a triangular blank. To make a triangular blank, set a table saw blade to 45° and cut halfway through a scrap block of wood, such as a 2x4. Cut from both directions to create a 45° angled groove in the middle. Slice halfway down the length of the board through the center of the groove with a band saw.

Clamp the angled jig to the band saw table. Position the square carving blank in the groove and feed the blank through the band saw blade to create two triangular blanks. Draw the wizard pattern lines and a centerline onto one of them.

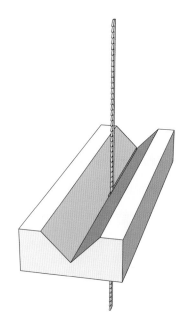

Outline the bottom of the hat. Make a mark on the corner 1½" (38mm) down from the top of the blank. Draw angled lines from the mark to the edges of the blank. Make ⅛" (3mm)-deep stop cuts along these lines.

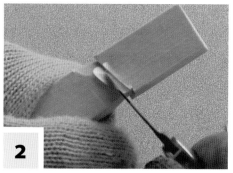

Relieve the face up to the hat. Start a slicing cut ¼" (6mm) down from the stop cut on each of the flat surfaces. Cut up to the stop cuts to create the surfaces for the eye sockets and cheeks.

Shape the face. Position the knife blade on the outside corners of the blank ¼" (6mm) down from the stop cut. Cut up to the stop cut to remove about ³⁄₁₆" (5mm) from both sides of the face.

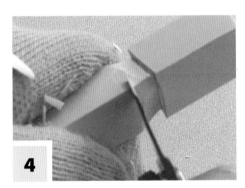

Define the bottom of the nose. Make a deep stop cut on the front corner, ½" (13mm) to ¾" (19mm) down from the bottom of the hat. Cut up to the stop cut from below to separate the bottom of the nose from the mouth and chin.

Outline the nose and eyes. Draw the nose and tops of the eyes. Starting at the inside corner of an eye, plunge the knife tip in and cut to the bottom of the nose. Start at the inside corner, and make a stop cut for each eye area.

Shape the nose and cheeks. Using the knife tip, cut up to the stop cuts made in Step 5 and remove a chip from each side of the nose. The deep areas where the cuts intersect will be the eye sockets. Remove the corners on the bottom of the nose.

Outline the mustache. Draw the hat, mustache, and beard. Angle the knife blade toward the mustache and make a stop cut around the mustache. Cut down toward the stop cut to separate the cheeks from the mustache.

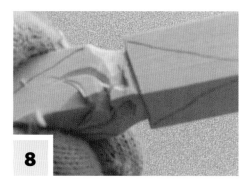

Shape the beard. Cut up to the stop cuts under the mustache. Cut along the beard outline to finish shaping the beard. If desired, go back with the tip of the knife and add hair lines and texture to the beard and mustache.

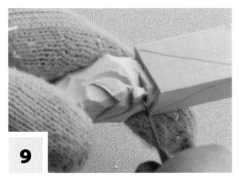

9

10

Shape the nose. Give the tip of the nose a rounded or pointed shape. Shave down the top to create the bridge of the nose. Cut up from the tip of the nose and free the chip by carving down from the eyebrows. Carve small semi-circles for the eyes.

Shape the hat. Use your thumb to push the back of the knife blade and roll the blade back toward you as you cut the hat to a point. You can make the hat long and pointed, squashed down, or even folded at the top. Use your imagination and make it your own.

Finishing

There are many ways you can finish the wizard—you can sand it to give it a more rounded look or leave it in a rustic or flat-plane style. Either way, scrub the carving with a denture brush, spray cleanser, and warm water to remove pencil marks or fuzzies. When dry, paint the carving with acrylic paint or stain it, if desired.

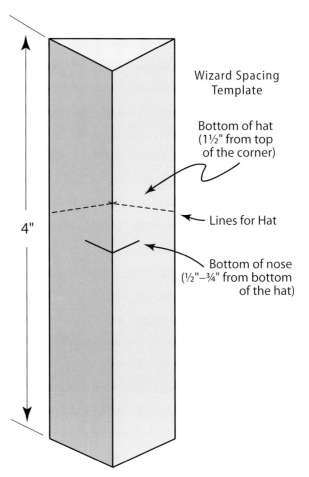

Wizard Spacing Template

Bottom of hat (1½" from top of the corner)

Lines for Hat

Bottom of nose (½"–¾" from bottom of the hat)

4"

Variations for 5-Minute Wizard

There are lots of ways you can adapt the 5-Minute Wizard to create other quick and easy projects. Experiment with different facial expressions, mustaches, beard shapes, and hat sizes. Toss out the hat and give the wizard a hood for a mysterious, magical look. Create a toothpick holder by drilling a small hole in the bottom of a wizard's beard. Glue a wizard onto a clothespin to spice up your laundry, hang photos, or keep papers organized. There are so many different options, which is why I love the 5-Minute Wizard. It's a project that just never gets old.

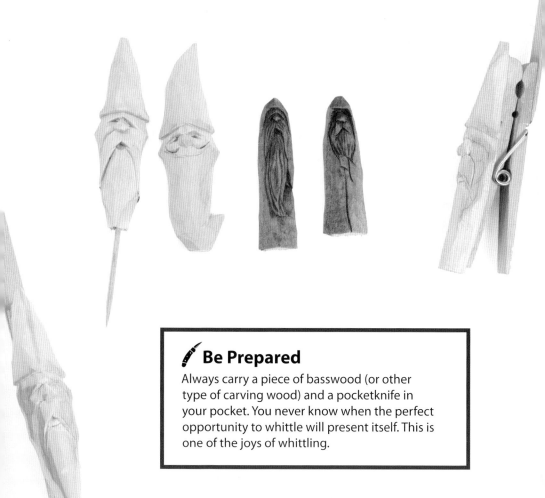

🔪 Be Prepared

Always carry a piece of basswood (or other type of carving wood) and a pocketknife in your pocket. You never know when the perfect opportunity to whittle will present itself. This is one of the joys of whittling.

Handcarved Christmas tree ornaments make special gifts. Santa ornaments do not need to be highly detailed to be recognizable. This quick and easy Santa can be completed in fifteen minutes flat. The project follows the same techniques used for the 5-Minute Wizard (page 24). With a few simple changes to the wizard, you'll have a tree full of Santa ornaments in no time!

The Santa is carved on a triangular blank. See page 25 for instructions on cutting a triangular blank. The corner of the blank is the centerline of Santa's face. Before starting to carve, sketch a few Santa faces. Your sketches should be about the same size as the one you will carve. Experiment with the shape of the mustache, beard, cheeks, and hat. When the mustache turns up, it looks like Santa is smiling.

Materials & Tools

Materials:
- Basswood:
  ¾" to 1" (19mm to 25mm) thick:
  1" x 6"
  (25mm x 152mm)
- Acrylic paint (optional)
- Stain and wood conditioner (optional)
- Polyurethane
- Small screw eye or pin back (optional)

Tools:
- Saws: table, band
- Knife
- V-tool
- Ruler

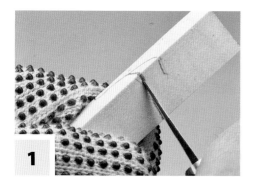

Outline the bottom of the hat and hat ball. Make a mark 1½" (38mm) down from the top on the corner of the blank. Draw an angled line from this point to the right side of the blank. Draw the fold of the hat and the round ball on the left. Make ⅛" (3mm)-deep stop cuts along these lines.

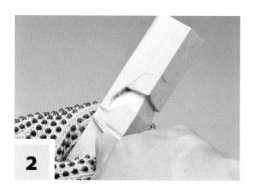

Separate the face from the hat. Start about ¼" (6mm) down from the stop cut at the bottom of the hat, and slice up to it to separate the face from the hat. Remove a chip from below the hat ball to separate it from the beard.

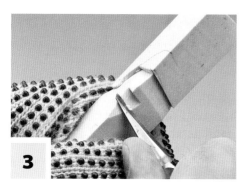

Define the bottom of the nose. Make a deep stop cut on the corner of the blank ¼" (6mm) down from the bottom of the hat. Cut up to this stop cut from below to separate the bottom of the nose from the mustache. Leave enough wood under the nose for the mustache.

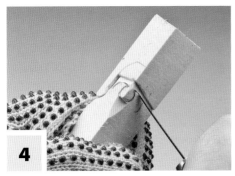

4

Rough out the nose and eyes. Draw the round nose and the tops of the eyes. Plunge the knife tip into the inside corner of one eye and cut down to the bottom of the nose. Do not undercut the nose. Plunge the tip of the knife into the inside corner of the eye and make a deep curved stop cut along the top of each eye socket. Repeat for the other eye.

5

Separate the nose from the cheeks. Cut up to the stop cuts made in Step 4 using the tip of the knife. Remove a chip from either side of the nose to separate the nose from the cheeks. This creates the eye cavities. Round the tip of the nose with a series of small cuts.

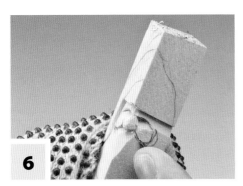

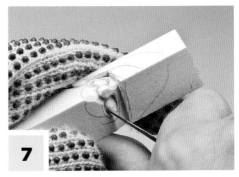

6

Separate the mustache and hat from the cheeks. Draw the mustache, beard, cheeks, and top of the hat. The top of the mustache forms circular cheek areas. Make curved stop cuts from the nose, across the top of the mustache, up to the stop cut at the top of the eyes.

7

Shape the cheeks. Round the cheeks down into the stop cuts defining the mustache and nose. Shave down the top of the nose to create the bridge.

8

Shape the bottom of the mustache.
Remove a small triangular wedge of wood from the corner of the blank at the bottom of the mustache for the mouth. Make a stop cut along the bottom of the mustache and cut up to it to separate the mustache from the beard.

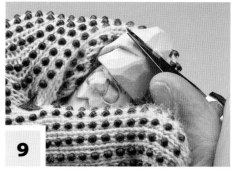

9

Shape the hat. Slice from the top of the hat to the bottom to remove the sharp corner. Slice up from the bottom and round the front and sides of the hat. Taper the hat toward the top. Use a push cut and curl the knife blade up and away from the hat toward the end of the cut. Remove a small wedge of wood from the bottom left side of the hat and shape the hat ball.

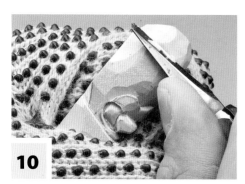

10

Shape the beard. Make paring cuts up and down (depending on the grain direction) to the pencil lines defining the beard. Round the bottom of the beard. Round any remaining flat, uncarved planes.

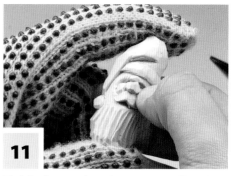

11

Finish the carving. Remove a small wedge or triangle of wood where the eyes will be painted. Make a ¹⁄₁₆" (2mm)-deep stop cut ¼" (6mm) above the bottom of the hat. Slice down to this stop cut to separate the hat band from the hat. You can texture the beard and mustache with a V-tool or leave them untextured. Use your thumbnail to press in the eyebrows.

Finishing

Decide whether you want to sand the Santa to have a more rounded look or leave the ornament in the rustic or flat-plane style. Either way, scrub the carving with a denture brush, spray cleanser, and warm water to remove pencil marks or fuzzies. When dry, paint the carving with acrylic paint or stain it. Attach a small screw eye to the top to form an ornament, or attach a pin back.

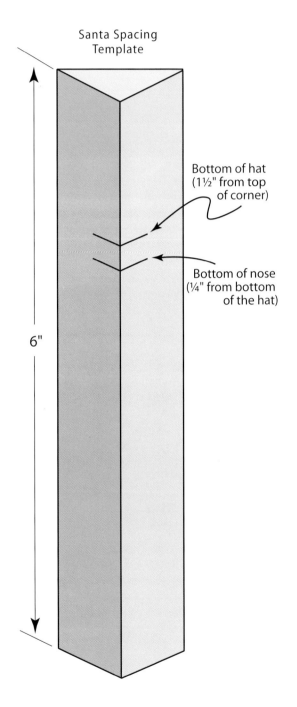

Santa Spacing Template

Bottom of hat
(1½" from top
of corner)

Bottom of nose
(¼" from bottom
of the hat)

6"

Here's an example of how you can finish your Santa carving.

Whittling can be as simplistic or as complex as we want to make it. Here's a little project that is both simplistic and fast, but has enough details to be impressive. You can also use the farmer blank to create different figures, such as a leprechaun, Uncle Sam, and a gnome.

I carved this piece from thicker wood as an in-the-round piece meant to sit on a shelf, but you can make a seasonal pin if you whittle it from ¼" (6mm)-thick stock and attach a pin back to the finished piece.

Getting Started

Trace the pattern onto the blank, and cut around the perimeter with a band saw, scroll saw, or coping saw. Draw the detail lines and a centerline onto the blank.

Materials & Tools

Materials:
- Basswood, ¾" (19mm) thick: 1" x 4" (25mm x 102mm)
- Sandpaper
- Acrylic paint (optional)
- Stain and wood conditioner (optional)
- Polyurethane

Tools:
- Saw: coping, band, or scroll
- Knife
- Paintbrushes (optional)

Outline the major elements. Make stop cuts along all of the detail lines. Deepen the stop cuts where the head and neck meet the chest, where the shoulders meet the neck in the back, at the bend in each arm, at the area in front of each ear, between the legs, at the pants pockets, and at the bottoms of the pants legs.

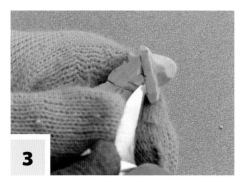

Rough in the hat. Make slicing cuts from the sides of the hat down to the hat brim, and then remove the sharp corners of the hat brim. Using thumb-assisted push cuts, round over the top of the hat.

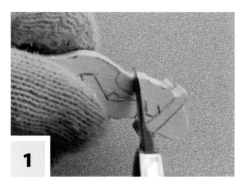

Shape the head. Remove chips from in front of and behind the ears. Narrow the sides of the face and forehead up to the bottom of the hat brim. Carve out a chip where the top of the arms, the head, and chest meet on each side. Carve out the back of the neck at the hairline.

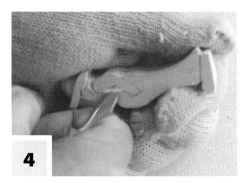

Shape the arms, chest, and belly. Carve out a chip where each arm bends. Make tapered slicing cuts up to the stop cuts that separate the arms from the chest and belly. Taper the top of the chest area to meet the neck area. Begin to round the chest and belly area.

Shape the legs and feet. Make V-shaped slicing cuts that angle into the stop cuts between the legs on the front and back. Make paring cuts on the feet up to the stop cuts at the bottoms of the pant legs. Make long slicing cuts to round the sides of the legs.

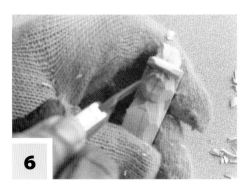

Add details to the face and head. Make deep stop cuts along the sides of the nose and across the tops of the eye areas. With the knife, remove the chips that are formed by these stop cuts on each side of the nose. Make a stop cut across the top of the nose, and slice up to it to shape and form the bridge of the nose. Then, make a shallow stop cut defining the top and bottom of the farmer's mustache, and pare down and up to these stop cuts.

7

8

Add details to the body. Round the arms down to the deep stop cuts that separate them from the body. Round the chest, belly, and legs into the stop cuts. Carve down to the stop cuts that define the farmer's overalls to separate them from the body. Carve to the stop cuts that define the front and back straps of the bib overalls. Remove a thin slice of wood from each forearm to make it appear that the hands are in the pockets.

Complete the carving. Carve the heels and taper the toes of the shoes. Remove a small divot inside each ear. Thin the brim of the hat.

You can carve so many different figures using this basic pattern. Carve a gnome, a hiker, leprechaun, or Uncle Sam.

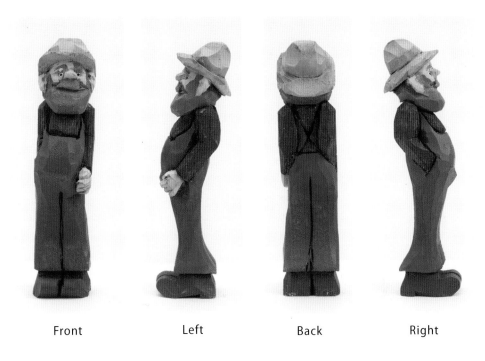

Front   Left   Back   Right

Farmer Pattern

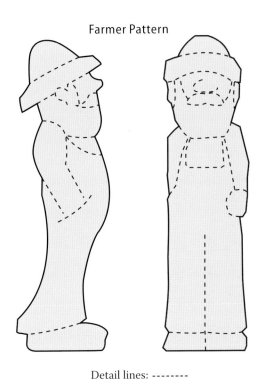

Finishing

I painted this figure with thinned acrylic paints. I sometimes burn a thin line between two colors to prevent the colors from bleeding into each other. Use a toothpick to apply the eye colors.

Detail lines: --------

One of the joys of carving with only a knife is that you can whittle just about anywhere. The blanks for these gnomes are small enough to carry in your pocket for whittling on the go. You can make this gnome into a figure or drill a hole in the bottom to create a bottle stopper.

Getting Started

Trace the side view of the pattern on the basswood, cut the blank, and draw the major features and the centerline. Drill a hole for a bottle stopper dowel, if desired. I glue the dowel into the blank before carving because it gives me something to hold as I carve.

Materials & Tools

Materials:
- Basswood, 1" (25mm) thick: 1" x 3½" (25mm x 89mm)
- Acrylic paint (optional)
- Polyurethane
- Finishing wax (optional)

Tools:
- Knife
- Saw: coping, band, or scroll
- Paintbrushes (optional)

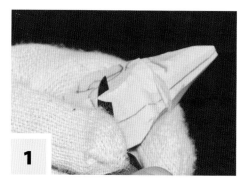

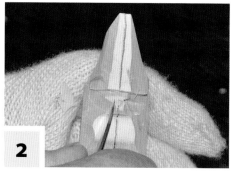

Rough out the head and hat. Whittle the hat to a point. Make a stop cut at the bottom of the hat. Start at the corners of the hat, and then cut at the front and back. Make stop cuts around the backs of the ears and remove slices of wood from behind the ears to make them protrude. Narrow the face and beard area.

Establish the nose and eyebrows. Plunge the knife tip vertically into the wood at the brow along the sides of the nose, and rock the blade down. Do not undercut the nose. Plunge the knife tip into the wood horizontally at the top of the nose and rock the blade out from the nose to form the eyebrow. Repeat for the other side.

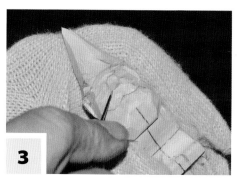

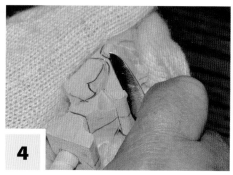

Rough out the face. Carve up to the stop cuts along the nose and eyebrows to remove the chips. Round the tip of the nose. Draw the mustache, and then make stop cuts above and below it. Carve down to the top of the mustache to separate it from the cheeks.

Separate the arms, legs, pockets, and beard. Make stop cuts along the shoulders, arms (front and back), pockets, and beard. Remove the chips from the inside corners of the elbows, the tops of the legs, and the bottom of the beard.

5

Narrow the face. Make a stop cut in front of each ear. Carve up to the stop cuts to separate the ears from the face and to narrow the sides of the face and the forehead.

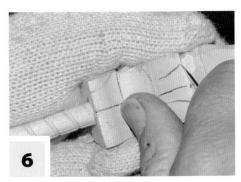

6

Shape the backs of the arms. Carve up to the stop cuts to separate the arms from the back.

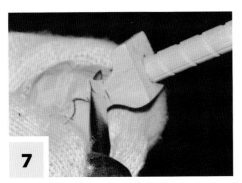

7

Shape the boots. Make stop cuts at the tops of the boots. Shape the legs down to the stop cuts. Then, round and refine the boots.

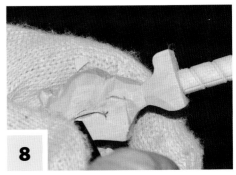

8

Refine the arms and legs. Carefully carve down to the stop cuts to refine the shapes of the arms and give them definition. To give the gnome a flat-plane look, just remove the hard edges of the arms and legs. Round the edges of the arms and legs for a softer look.

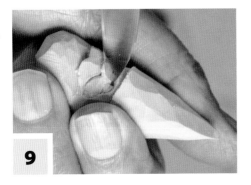

9

Carve the eyes. Make stop cuts in a diamond pattern along the top and bottom eyelids. Then, shave up to the stop cuts to remove the chips, leaving a slight point in the middle of each eye to represent the eyeball. You could also leave the eye sockets flat and paint the eyes.

10

Finish the gnome. Use a knife to texture the beard and hair. Using a stiff brush, such as a denture brush, scrub the carving with soap and water. Allow it to dry, and then apply stain or wax, or paint it with acrylic paints.

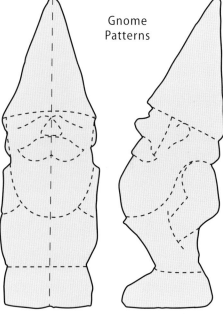

Gnome Patterns

Detail lines: --------

Emphasizing Features

To make the features stand out, remove small triangular chips wherever two surfaces come together—the bottom sides of the nose and cheeks, the backs of the ears, and the insides of the elbows.

Front   Side   Back

If a dog is man's best friend, this project is a carver's best friend! These whittled dogs are excellent for beginners, as well as more experienced carvers, because you can decide the amount of detail to add.

For this project, I whittled a German shepherd, but I've also whittled a boxer, a poodle, and a Scottish terrier. If you'd like to carve a different breed, find a good profile illustration with just enough detail. Scan the illustration into a computer and reduce or enlarge it to create your own pattern. Refer to the illustration or a photograph of the dog breed as you carve.

Materials & Tools

Materials:
- Basswood, ¾" (19mm) thick: 2½" x 3¼" (64mm x 83mm)
- Sandpaper
- Acrylic paint (optional)
- Stain and wood conditioner (optional)
- Polyurethane

Tools:
- Saw: coping, band, or scroll
- Knife
- Paintbrushes (optional)

Getting Started

Trace the pattern onto the blank, and cut around the perimeter with a band saw, scroll saw, or coping saw. Draw the detail lines and a centerline onto the blank.

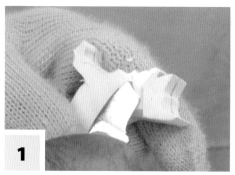

1

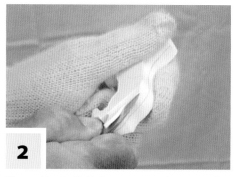

2

Carve the neck. Make a stop cut between the head and the neck area. Narrow the neck area toward the centerline.

Carve the tail. Make a stop cut between the tail and the dog's hindquarters. Narrow the tail toward the centerline.

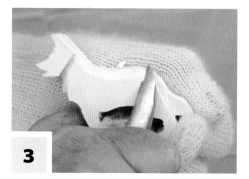

3

Shape the back and belly. Continue narrowing and shaping the dog's tail, back, and neck toward the centerline. Stop-cut between the legs and belly. Narrow the belly between the rear and front legs.

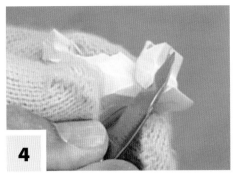

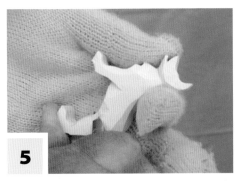

4

Carve the head. Narrow the dog's head toward the snout. Remove the wood between the ears. Round the snout, and define the mouth.

5

Shape the dog's legs. Narrow the legs and shape the paws. Leave the legs connected for stability and a folk-art feel.

Front   Side   Back

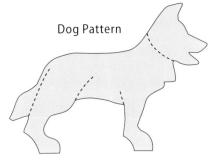

Dog Pattern

Detail lines: - - - - - - - -

Finishing

There are several ways to finish the dog: sand it smooth, leave the knife cuts visible in a flat-plane style, stain it, or paint it. Mix and match these finishing techniques or leave the dog unfinished.

Bears are one of the fiercest—and cutest—animals out there. Native Americans often saw them as a sign of strength and wisdom. This majestic animal would be a great gift for a child or adult.

Getting Started

Transfer the pattern to the blank and cut around the perimeter with a band saw, scroll saw, or coping saw. Draw detail lines and a centerline onto the blank.

Stay Symmetrical

As you carve the bear, keep turning the blank in your hands to make the same cuts on each side. This will keep the piece symmetrical. Turning the blank may also be necessary to be sure that you whittle "down hill," or with the grain.

Materials & Tools

Materials:
- Basswood, ¾" (19mm) thick: 3½" x 2" (89mm x 51mm)
- Sandpaper
- Acrylic paint (optional)
- Stain and wood conditioner (optional)
- Polyurethane

Tools:
- Saw: coping, band, or scroll
- Knife
- Paintbrushes (optional)

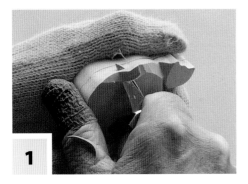

1

Carve the head and back. I suggest selecting a thicker piece of wood for the bear, because bears are heavier animals. Make a stop cut between the bear's head and neck. Narrow the head and neck to this stop cut, making sure to shape both the head and neck toward the centerline. Round the bear's back and rump toward the centerline with paring cuts and thumb-assisted slicing push cuts.

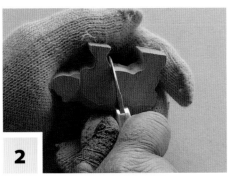

2

Shape the belly. Make stop cuts between the front legs and the belly, and then between the rear legs and the belly. Narrow, round, and shape the belly between these stop cuts.

3

Define the head. Narrow and shape the bear's head in proportion to its body, and taper it toward the nose. Round the nose area.

4

Shape the bear's legs. Narrow the legs slightly and shape the paws. You can leave the legs connected or split them.

5

Define the ears. Split and shape the ears and round the nose area. Finish rounding the bear's back, belly, neck, head and legs.

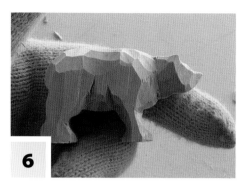

6

Finish the bear. It may be necessary to scrub the bear with a stiff brush (such as a denture brush), warm water, and liquid detergent to remove pencil marks, dirt, or wood "fuzzies" at the bottoms of cuts. If you scrub the piece, let it dry before applying a finish.

Front   Side   Back

Finishing

There are several ways to finish the bear: sand it smooth, leave the knife cuts visible in a flat-plane style, stain it, or paint it. Mix and match these finishing techniques or leave the bear unfinished. See the Finishing section in the Appendix (page 92) for more information. I chose to paint the bear's body brown.

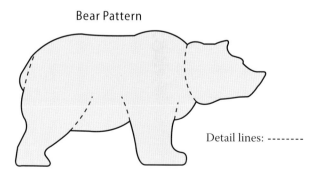

Bear Pattern

Detail lines: --------

Gargoyle

Gargoyles have been carved for millennia. The original designs were hollow and functioned as waterspouts—their long necks or bodies channeled rainwater away from the masonry. Gargoyles can take the shape of animals, people, and monsters; most are scary-looking and are said to protect their buildings with their frightening appearances. Decorative designs like this one, which aren't intended for use as spouts, are technically called grotesques.

By resizing the pattern and adjusting the thickness of the basswood blank, you can carve this pattern any size. My original is 1" (25mm) tall and uses a ¾" (19mm)-thick blank. For a 1½" (38mm)- to 2" (51mm)-tall gargoyle, use 1" (25mm)-thick basswood so the wings can flare out from the body.

Getting Started

Trace the pattern onto the blank, and cut around the perimeter with a band saw, scroll saw, or coping saw. Leave a handle on the bottom of the blank to make it easier to hold. Draw centerlines on the edges of the blank, and draw the head, body, legs, and wings.

Materials & Tools

Materials:
- Basswood, ¾" (19mm) thick: 1" x 1" (25mm x 25mm)
- Sandpaper
- Acrylic paint (optional)

Tools:
- Saw: coping, band, or scroll
- Knife
- Paintbrushes (optional)
- Rotary tool with bits: ¾" (19mm)-diameter sanding drum, ¼" (6mm)-diameter sanding drum (optional)

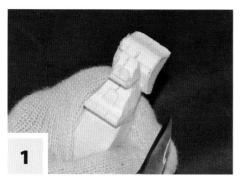

1

Rough out the head and body. Make a stop cut between the head and the wings. Use a knife to separate and narrow the head. Narrow the body from the shoulders to the bottom of the legs. This narrowing allows the wings to extend beyond the body.

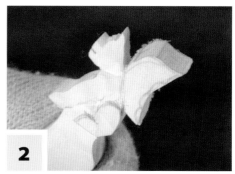

2

Rough out the legs. Make stop cuts around the legs on both sides. Carve to these cuts to isolate the legs. Make deeper stop cuts where the rear legs bend, and remove the triangular chips at these bends.

3

Separate the front and back legs. Make stop cuts along the insides of the legs on the front and back. Carve to these cuts to separate the legs and isolate them from the gargoyle's belly and back.

4

Carve the face. Carve a narrow horizontal V-groove for the mouth, and carve the sides of the muzzle back to the brow bones. Carve a groove to separate the ears. Pay attention to the grain direction, and use a soft touch with a sharp knife. Smooth and slightly round the eye area, and use the tip of the knife to carve small holes for the eyes.

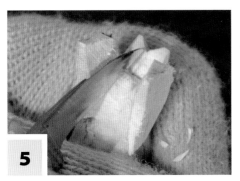

5

Separate the wings. Make a stop cut at the top and bottom center of the wings, and then slice down from the sides of the wings to this stop cut. Continue deepening the stop cut and removing wood from both sides down to the stop cut. It is best to use a paring cut that curls the chip away to leave a rounded bottom between the wings. Be careful not to put any pressure on the wings; they snap easily.

6

Refine the wings. Scallop the edges of the wings. Carve these scallops before thinning the wings. Round the fronts of the wings, and then round the front and rear legs.

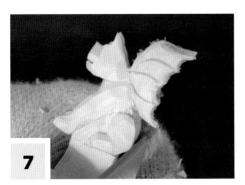

7

Carve the wing veins. Draw veins from the tips of the scallops to the base of each wing. Carve V-grooves along these lines. For more texture, carefully carve out the areas between the veins.

8

Finish the wings. Thin the wings with the knife or sandpaper. Be careful, because the wings are fragile at the base. Cut off the handle.

✏ Easy Wing Shaping

If you prefer, use a rotary tool with a ¾" (19mm)-diameter sanding drum and sleeve to divide the wings. To scallop the wing edges, use the rotary tool and a ¼" (6mm)-diameter sanding drum or a piece of sandpaper wrapped around a piece of dowel.

Front

Side

Back

Gargoyle Patterns

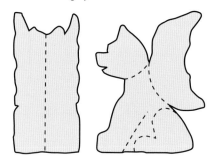

Detail lines: --------

Finishing

There are several ways to finish the gargoyle: sand it smooth, leave the knife cuts visible in a flat-plane style, stain it, or paint it. Mix and match these finishing techniques or leave the gargoyle unfinished. See the Finishing section in the Appendix (page 92) for more information. Thinned gray acrylic paint makes the gargoyle look like it's carved from stone.

Horses are always a favorite among children and adults. Once you get enough practice, you can make a whole herd of horses for kids– and kids at heart–to play with!

Make sure you use the pattern and check your work against the photos to ensure you whittle the correct characteristics for the horse. For example, it could get confused with a dog if you don't make the neck long enough and the tail thick enough.

Getting Started

Trace the pattern onto the blank, and cut around the perimeter with a band saw, scroll saw, or coping saw. Draw the detail lines and a centerline onto the blank.

Materials & Tools

Materials:
- Basswood, ¾ (19mm) thick: 3" x 3" (76mm x 76mm)
- Acrylic paints (optional)
- Stain and wood conditioner (optional)
- Polyurethane

Tools:
- Saw: coping, band or scroll
- Knife
- Paintbrushes (optional)

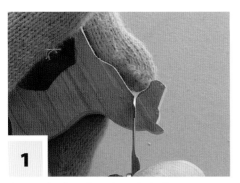

1

Carve the head and neck. Make a stop cut between the head and the neck. Begin to narrow the neck toward the stop cut and the centerline.

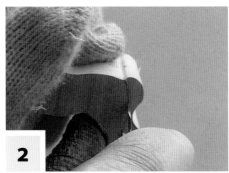

2

Carve the tail. Make stop cuts between the tail and the horse's hindquarters. Narrow and round the tail toward these stop cuts, the centerline of the tail, and the tip of the tail.

3

Shape the body of the horse. Narrow and shape the tail, back, and neck toward the centerline. Narrow the horse's head in proportion to its body, and taper it toward the muzzle. Split the ears and round the muzzle.

Remove Chips Easily

When removing small chips and slices of wood, use just the tip of a very sharp knife.

Shape the belly. Make stop cuts between the front legs and the belly, and then between the rear legs and the belly. Begin to narrow and round the belly between these stop cuts.

Shape the horse's legs. Narrow the legs and shape the hooves. Leave the legs connected or split them; I chose to leave the legs connected for stability.

Finish the horse. It may be necessary to scrub the horse with a stiff brush (such as a denture brush), warm water, and liquid detergent to remove pencil marks, dirt, or wood "fuzzies" at the bottoms of cuts. If you scrub the piece, let it dry before applying a finish.

Front   Side   Back

Finishing

There are several ways to finish the horse: sand it smooth, leave the knife cuts visible in a flat-plane style, stain it, or paint it. Mix and match these finishing techniques or leave the horse unfinished. See the Finishing section in the Appendix (page 92) for more information. I chose to paint the horse with thinned brown paint.

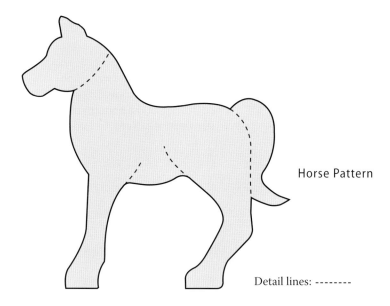

Horse Pattern

Detail lines: --------

Fox

Are you as sly as a fox? In fables, the fox is always portrayed as crafty and cunning, but I can't help thinking they're cute! I've heard before that foxes are so good at hiding that if you see one, it's only because it let you see it.

Getting Started

Trace the pattern onto the blank, and cut the perimeter with a band saw, scroll saw, or coping saw. Draw the detail lines and a centerline onto the blank.

Materials & Tools

Materials:
- Basswood, ¾ (19mm) thick: 2 x 2 (51mm x 51mm)
- Acrylic paints (optional)
- Stain and wood conditioner (optional)
- Polyurethane

Tools:
- Saw: coping, band or scroll
- Knife
- Paintbrushes (optional)

Carve the head. Make stop cuts where the head joins the neck, and remove wood up to these stop cuts.

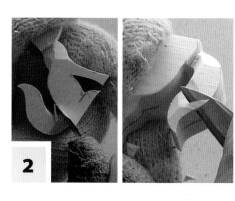

Carve the tail. Make stop cuts where the tail meets the rear of the fox. Remove wood from the tail and the fox's rear up to these stop cuts. Round the sides of the tail and the tip of the tail to the centerline.

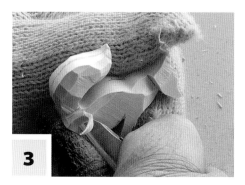

Shape the back. Begin to narrow and round the sides of the fox's back toward the centerline.

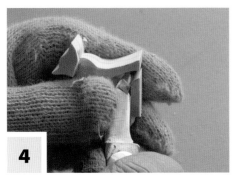

4

Carve the legs. Make stop cuts at the tops of the fox's back legs, where they meet the body. Remove chips up to these stop cuts. Repeat for the front legs.

5

Narrow the back. Continue narrowing the fox's back, belly, and neck toward the centerline.

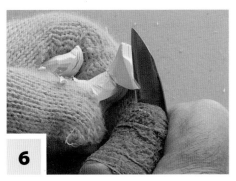

6

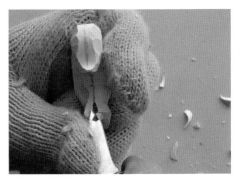

Define the head. Narrow the fox's head in proportion to its body. Make sure to taper the face toward the nose. Then, separate and shape the ears.

✏ Remove Small Chips

Avoid "hogging" off large amounts of wood with one cut, which may split off too much wood. A helpful carver once told me to think "grains of rice" when removing wood with a knife.

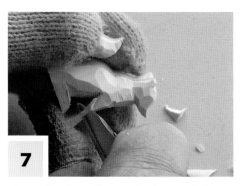

7

Shape the legs. Narrow the legs and shape the paws. Take thin slices from the edges of the legs.

8

Finish the fox. It may be necessary to scrub the fox with a stiff brush (such as a denture brush), warm water, and liquid detergent to remove pencil marks, dirt, or wood "fuzzies" at the bottom of cuts. If you scrub the piece, let it dry before applying a finish.

Prevent Breakage

You may find that, due to the wood grain direction, the fox's tail is a little weak and could break. Use caution as you whittle the fox's tail, and when you have finished it, apply cyanoacrylate (CA) glue, such as Super Glue, to the place where the tail meets the body.

Front   Side   Back

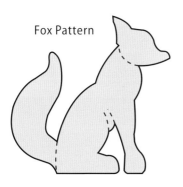

Fox Pattern

Detail lines: --------

Finishing

There are several ways to finish the fox: sand it smooth, leave the knife cuts visible in a flat-plane style, stain it, or paint it. Mix and match these finishing techniques or leave the fox unfinished. See the Finishing section in the Appendix (page 92) for more information. I chose to paint the fox's body orange; its feet, eyes, nose, and outer ears black; and its chin, stomach, and the tip of its tail white.

Fawns are the epitome of innocence! They are cute and always a favorite with children. If you give the fawn to a child, know that it may receive some rough play. Don't make the legs or ears too thin, as they may break off and pose a hazard to the child, depending on his or her age.

Baby animals are usually tiny projects, so I suggest leaving a "handle" of wood attached to the fawn's hind legs to make the blank easier to hold while you carve. You will cut this off when you're done, of course.

Getting Started

Trace the pattern onto the blank, and cut the perimeter with a band saw, scroll saw, or coping saw. Draw the detail lines and a centerline onto the blank.

Materials & Tools

Materials:
- Basswood, ⅜" (10mm) thick: 2 x 4 (51mm x 102mm)
- Acrylic paints (optional)
- Stain and wood conditioner (optional)
- Polyurethane

Tools:
- Saw: coping, band or scroll
- Knife
- Paintbrushes (optional)

Carve the head and neck. Make stop cuts between the fawn's head and neck. Begin to narrow the neck and head to these stop cuts and toward the centerline.

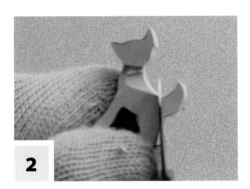

Carve the back and tail. Make stop cuts around the base of the fawn's tail. Make paring cuts down and up to these stop cuts to round the rump and tail to the centerline. Make paring cuts to bring the tail to a point.

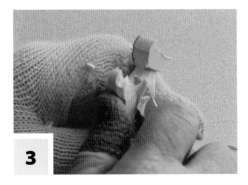

Shape the back. Round the fawn's back and rump toward the centerline. Continue narrowing the tail and neck toward the centerline.

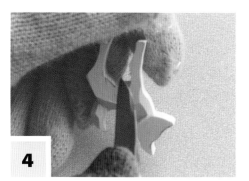

Shape the belly. Make stop cuts between the front legs and the belly, and then between the rear legs and the belly. Begin to narrow, round, and shape the belly between these stop cuts.

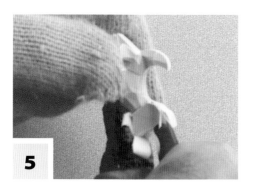

Define the head. Narrow and shape the fawn's head in proportion to its body, and taper the head toward the nose.

Shape the legs. If the fawn is intended for children it may be best to leave the legs connected. Children won't notice the difference, and it adds strength to the legs.

7

8

Define the ears. Split and shape the ears. Continue rounding the fawn's back, belly, neck, head, and legs.

Finish the fawn. Cut the handle off with a saw of your choice. It may be necessary to scrub the fawn with a stiff brush (such as a denture brush), warm water, and liquid detergent to remove pencil marks, dirt, or wood "fuzzies" at the bottoms of cuts. If you scrub the piece, let it dry before applying a finish.

✎ Remedy for Difficult-To-Carve Basswood

Basswood is a good wood to whittle, because it is not grainy and it holds detail well. But not all basswood is the same. When whittling harder basswood, spray a mix of 50-50 water and rubbing alcohol onto the wood and let it absorb. This will make the wood easier to whittle.

Front   Side   Back

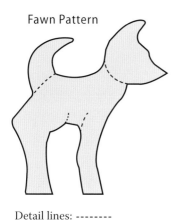

Fawn Pattern

Detail lines: --------

Finishing

There are several ways to finish the fawn: sand it smooth, leave the knife cuts visible in a flat-plane style, stain it, or paint it. Mix and match these finishing techniques or leave the fawn unfinished. See the Finishing section in the Appendix (page 92) for more information. I chose to paint the fawn's body brown with white spots to indicate its age. I painted the bottom of the tail and eyes white and the pupils black.

Piglet

Pigs often get a bad rap as being smelly and dirty, but who can resist a piglet? Have fun carving this teeny animal. I suggest leaving a handle of wood on the piglet's front legs, which will make carving much easier.

Getting Started

Trace the pattern onto the blank, and cut around the perimeter with a band saw, scroll saw, or coping saw. Draw the detail lines and a centerline onto the blank.

Materials & Tools

Materials:
- Basswood, ½" (13mm) thick: 2" x 3" (51mmx 76mm)
- Acrylic paints (optional)
- Stain and wood conditioner (optional)
- Polyurethane

Tools:
- Saw: coping, band or scroll
- Knife
- Paintbrushes (optional)

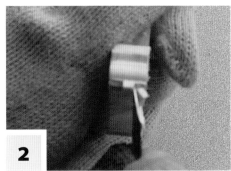

Carve the head. Make stop cuts between the piglet's head and neck. Narrow the neck and head to these stop cuts and toward the centerline.

Carve the tail. Make stop cuts around the sides of the piglet's tail. Use paring cuts to narrow the tail and round the rump to the centerline between the stop cuts.

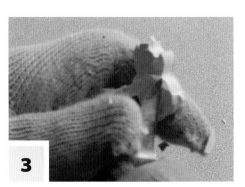

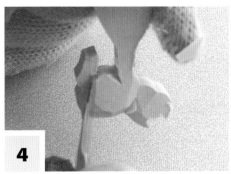

Shape the back. Round the piglet's back and rump toward the centerline.

Shape the belly. Make stop cuts between the front legs and the belly, and then between the rear legs and the belly. Narrow, round, and shape the belly between these stop cuts.

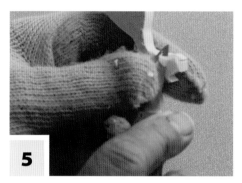

5

Define the head. Narrow and shape the piglet's head in proportion to its body, and taper the head toward the nose. Be sure to leave the piglet's nose flat on the end.

6

Shape the legs. Narrow the legs and, if you prefer, shape the hooves. I left the feet unshaped. If the piglet is intended for children, I advise leaving the legs connected for strength and durability.

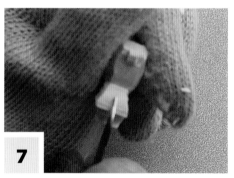

7

Define the ears. Split and shape the ears to points. Continue rounding the piglet's back, belly, neck, head, and legs.

8

Finish the piglet. Cut the handle off with a saw of your choice. It may be necessary to scrub the pig with a stiff brush (such as a denture brush), warm water, and liquid detergent to remove pencil marks, dirt, or wood "fuzzies" at the bottom of cuts. If you scrub the piece, let it dry before applying a finish.

Front

Side

Back

Piglet Pattern

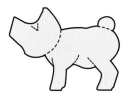

Detail lines:

Finishing

There are several ways to finish the piglet: sand it smooth, leave the knife cuts visible in a flat-plane style, stain it, or paint it. Mix and match these finishing techniques or leave the piglet unfinished. See the Finishing section in the Appendix (page 92) for more information. I chose to paint the pig's body pink, its eyes white, and its pupils black.

The baby fox is another crowd favorite. Did you know that baby foxes are technically called "kits"? They are born blind, deaf, and toothless, but they head out of their den and into the world within three weeks!

Getting Started

Trace the pattern onto the blank, and cut the perimeter with a band saw, scroll saw, or coping saw. Draw the detail lines and a centerline onto the blank.

Materials & Tools

Materials:
- Basswood, ½" (13mm) thick: 2" x 3" (51mmx 76mm)
- Acrylic paints (optional)
- Stain and wood conditioner (optional)
- Polyurethane

Tools:
- Saw: coping, band or scroll
- Knife
- Paintbrushes (optional)

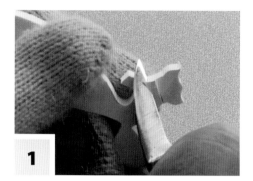

Carve the head. Make stop cuts between the fox's head and neck. Narrow the neck and head to the stop cuts and toward the centerline.

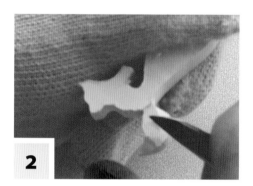

Carve the tail. Make stop cuts around the base of the fox's tail. Use paring cuts to round the rump and tail to the centerline between the stop cuts. Bring the tail to a point with paring cuts.

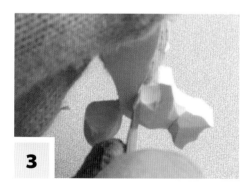

Shape the back and belly. Make stop cuts between the front legs and the belly, and then between the rear legs and the belly. Narrow, round, and shape the belly between these stop cuts. Round the fox's back and rump toward the centerline.

4

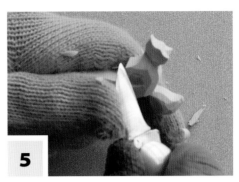

5

Define the head. Narrow the fox's head toward its nose, keeping the head in proportion with the body. Round the nose.

Shape the fox's legs. Narrow the legs and shape the paws. You can separate the legs, or leave them connected for stability.

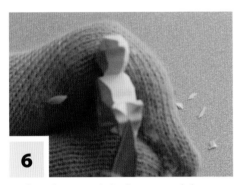

6

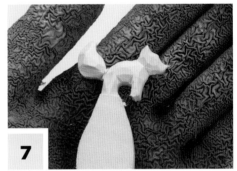

7

Define the ears. Split the ears and shape them to a point. Continue rounding of the fox's back, belly, neck, head, and legs toward the centerline.

Finish the fox. Cut the handle off with a saw of your choice. It may be necessary to scrub the fox with a stiff brush (such as a denture brush), warm water, and liquid detergent to remove pencil marks, dirt, or wood "fuzzies" at the bottom of cuts. If you scrub the piece, let it dry before applying a finish.

Is Your Blade Sharp Enough?

There are several ways to determine if a knife blade is really sharp. I like to place the cutting edge of the blade at a 90° angle to my thumbnail and move the blade against it. If the blade slides across without digging in, it may need to be stropped.

Front   Side   Back

Fox Pattern

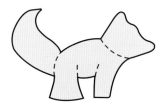

Detail lines: --------

Finishing

There are several ways to finish the baby fox: sand it smooth, leave the knife cuts visible in a flat-plane style, stain it, or paint it. Mix and match these finishing techniques or leave the baby fox unfinished. See the Finishing section in the Appendix (page 92) for more information. I chose to paint the baby fox orange; the tip of its tail, stomach, eyes, neck, ears, and lower face white; and its feet, nose, and pupils black.

Here's a bear cub to keep the mama (or papa) bear company (see page 47). Notice how his mouth is open, unlike the adult bear—that's because he's ready to play!

Getting Started

Trace the pattern onto the blank, and cut around the perimeter with a band saw, scroll saw, or coping saw. Draw the detail lines and a centerline onto the blank.

Materials & Tools

Materials:
- Basswood, ¾" (19mm) thick: 2" x 3" (51mmx 76mm)
- Acrylic paints (optional)
- Stain and wood conditioner (optional)
- Polyurethane

Tools:
- Saw: coping, band or scroll
- Knife
- Paintbrushes (optional)

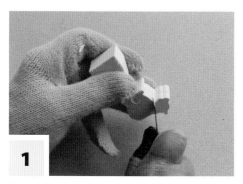

1

Carve the head and neck. Make stop cuts between the cub's head and neck. Then, narrow the neck and head to these stop cuts, and toward the centerline.

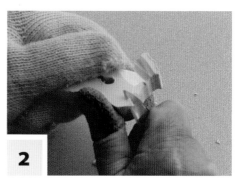

2

Shape the back. Round the cub's back and rump toward the centerline.

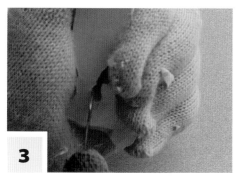

3

Shape the belly. Make stop cuts between the front legs and the belly, and then between the rear legs and the belly. Narrow, round, and shape the belly between these stop cuts.

4

Define the head and face. Continue to narrow and shape the cub's head in proportion to its body. Taper the head toward the nose. Then, round the nose and define the mouth.

Shape the legs and feet. You can separate the legs, or leave them connected for stability. If the bear cub is intended for children, it may be best to leave the legs attached. Children won't notice, and it adds strength to the legs.

Define the ears. Split the ears and round them. If needed, continue to round the cub's back, belly, neck, head, and legs.

Finish the bear cub. Cut the handle off with a saw of your choice. It may be necessary to scrub the piece with a stiff brush (such as a denture brush), warm water, and liquid detergent to remove pencil marks, dirt, or wood "fuzzies" at the bottom of cuts. If you scrub it, let it dry before applying a finish.

| Front | Side | Back |

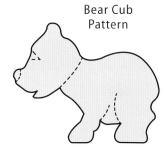

Bear Cub
Pattern

Detail lines: --------

Finishing

There are several ways to finish the bear cub: sand it smooth, leave the knife cuts visible in a flat-plane style, stain it, or paint it. Mix and match these finishing techniques or leave the bear cub unfinished. See the Finishing section in the Appendix (page 92) for more information. I chose to paint the bear cub brown, its eyes white, and its pupils black.

✒ The Nature of Whittling

A warning about the nature of whittling: You can become so engrossed in your whittling that time seems to stand still. Many seek this state of (un)consciousness. However, it can get you in trouble. Sitting in the backyard, lost in my whittling, I have missed activities that should not have been missed, like dinner, doctor's appointments, and picking my wife up at the airport!

In Indian culture, the elephant is considered lucky. Whittle these adorable pieces for your friends and family—and keep one for yourself!

Getting Started

Trace the pattern onto the blank, and cut around the perimeter with a band saw, scroll saw, or coping saw. Draw the detail lines and a centerline onto the blank.

Materials & Tools

Materials:
- Basswood, ¾" (19mm) thick: 3" x 3½" (76mm x 89mm)
- Acrylic paints (optional)
- Stain and wood conditioner (optional)
- Polyurethane

Tools:
- Saw: coping, band or scroll
- Knife
- Paintbrushes (optional)

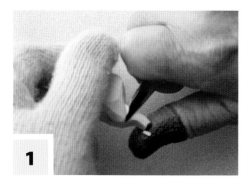

Carve the trunk. With paring cuts, taper and round the elephant's trunk toward the tip, the top of its head, and the centerline.

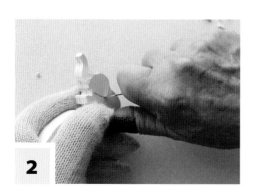

Carve the ears. Make stop cuts at the lines defining the elephant's ears, sides, and the top. Using paring cuts, remove wood up to these stop cuts.

Shape the tail and back. Make shallow stop cuts at the sides of the elephant's tail, and remove some thin slices of wood to these stop cuts to make the tail stand out from the rump. Begin to round the elephant's back and rump toward the centerline.

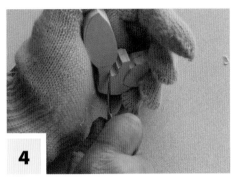

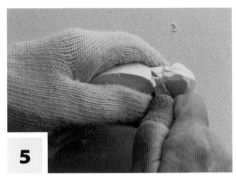

4

5

Define the legs and belly. Make stop cuts between the front legs and the belly, and then between the rear legs and the belly. Narrow, round, and shape the belly between these stop cuts.

Shape the legs. Narrow the legs and shape the feet. You can separate the legs, or leave them connected for stability.

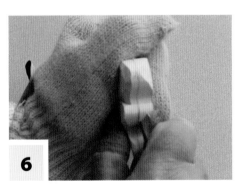

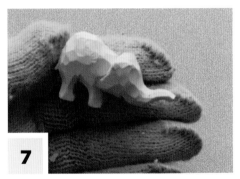

6

7

Define the ears. On top of the head, separate the ears. Round the elephant's back, belly, neck, head, and legs.

Finish the baby elephant. Cut the handle off with a saw of your choice. It may be necessary to scrub the elephant with a stiff brush (such as a denture brush), warm water, and liquid detergent to remove pencil marks, dirt, or wood "fuzzies" at the bottom of cuts. If you scrub the piece, let it dry before applying a finish.

Front

Side

Back

Baby Elephant Pattern

Detail lines: --------

Finishing

There are several ways to finish the baby elephant: sand it smooth, leave the knife cuts visible in a flat-plane style, stain it, or paint it. Mix and match these finishing techniques or leave the baby elephant unfinished. See the Finishing section in the Appendix (page 92) for more information. I chose to paint the elephant gray, its eyes white, and its pupils black.

✎ Finger Protection

Some whittlers use a wrap around their thumbs and fingers as a protection from nicks. When demonstrating whittling to some children, I used some red wrap on my thumb and fingers. After noticing that the children were extremely attentive, I asked one how he enjoyed the demonstration. All he mentioned was the "blood" soaking through the bandage on my thumb. I learned not to use a red thumb wrap—blue or green is much better.

Appendix

On the following pages, you'll find information on safety, basic cuts to make in whittling, sharpening your knife, and finishing your projects. Refer to this section again and again to keep your whittling skills as sharp as your knife!

Safety

There is risk involved whenever you handle sharp tools. A knife sharp enough to cut through wood will easily cut skin. Most cuts are small nicks that heal quickly and don't leave a scar. However, it's best to follow simple safety procedures to prevent serious injuries.

The fundamental rule when it comes to whittling is to be aware not only of where the blade *is*, but also where the blade *could*

Wear a glove on the hand holding your carving.

go. Wood can change density at any point, and you need to change the amount of pressure you apply to the knife accordingly. Imagine pushing hard to cut through a knot, only to find a softer section of wood beyond. The sharp edge will quickly slice through the softer area and cut into whatever is on the other side. The knife doesn't care if it's open air, a carving bench, or your hand.

Boy Scouts are taught to always cut away from themselves. While this is good advice, there are times when you cut toward your thumb, such as when making a paring cut (see page 86). When making a paring cut, wear a leather thumb protector, wrap your thumb with cloth tape, or position your thumb far enough down on the project that the knife won't hit your thumb if it slips.

Because most cuts occur on the hand holding the project, carvers often wear a cut-resistant glove on that hand. It is possible to prevent cuts by being aware of where the sharp edge can (and probably will) go. Always cut away from yourself when you are removing bark or large amounts of wood. When you are carving finer details, anchor your holding hand to the carving hand. Place the thumb of your holding hand on the back of the thumb on the knife-holding hand when doing a push cut. Or, rest the fingers of your knife hand on the fingers of your holding hand. Anchoring your hands adds stability and control, making it less likely that the knife will slip.

Wear a thumb guard when cutting toward your thumb.

Some whittlers use their thighs as carving benches. A cut on your thigh can be serious. Carving on a workbench or table is recommended. If you cut toward your thigh, invest in a strip of leather to protect your leg.

Without proper precautions, a slip of the knife can result in an emergency-room visit. Follow these simple safety rules and you'll never require anything more than a Band-Aid.

Cut away from yourself to prevent injury.

✎ Whittling in Public

When whittling in public places, be sure to check with the folks in charge. This may be security in a public shopping mall. You may imagine what could happen if you are whittling in a public mall and someone reports to mall security that there is a person with a knife.

Basic Cuts

Like most types of carving (woodcarving, ice carving, stone carving), whittling is a subtractive art—you remove all of the material that isn't part of your vision for the final piece. For example, to carve a dog, remove all of the wood that doesn't contribute to the shape of the dog.

Most whittlers use four basic cuts to remove excess wood: the push cut, the paring cut, the stop cut, and the V-shaped cut. Master these four basic types of cuts and you'll be ready to tackle a multitude of projects.

Stop Cut

As the name suggests, the stop cut is used to create a hard line at the end of another cut. Your hand position depends on the placement of the cut you need to make. Simply cut straight into the wood to create a stop cut. Make a stop cut first to prevent a consecutive cut from extending beyond the intended area. Make a stop cut second to free a chip of wood remaining from a primary cut.

Push Cut

For the push cut, hold the wood in one hand. Hold the knife in your other hand with your thumb on the back of the blade. Push the knife through the wood, away from your body. This type of cut is also called a "straightaway" cut. For additional control or power, place the thumb of the wood-holding hand on top of the thumb on the blade, and use the wood-holding thumb as a pivot as you rotate the wrist of your knife-holding hand. This maneuver is often called the "thumb-pushing," or "lever," cut.

Paring Cut

The paring cut gives you a great deal of control but requires you to cut toward your thumb. Wear a thumb protector or be aware of where the knife could cut at all times, especially if it slips beyond the anticipated stopping point. To perform the paring cut, which is also called the "draw" cut, hold the wood in one hand. Hold the knife in the other hand with four fingers. The cutting edge points toward your thumb. Rest the thumb of your knife-holding hand on the wood behind the area you want to carve. Extend the thumb as much as possible. Close your hand, pulling the knife toward your thumb, to slice through the wood. This is the same action used to peel (or pare) potatoes.

V-Shaped Cut

To make a V-shaped cut, hold a knife as described for a paring cut. Anchor the thumb of the knife hand against the wood and cut in at an angle with the tip of the knife. Rotate the wood, anchor your thumb on the other side of the cut, and cut in at an angle, running beside the first cut. Angle the two cuts so the bottom or deepest part of the cuts meet in the center. This creates a V-shaped groove. Use the center of the cutting edge to make intersecting angled cuts on the corner of a blank, creating V-shaped notches.

✒ Slicing vs. Push Cuts

Thumb-assisted push cuts that use the knife to make a slight slicing motion will generally remove wood with less effort, but require more experience and practice. However, sometimes the easiest way to whittle is to make push cuts with a well-honed knife blade, especially to achieve fine detail with the tip of the blade.

Basics of Sharpening

Although it may seem contradictory, a sharp knife is a safe knife. When a knife is dull, or not shaped properly, it requires more force to push the blade through the wood. The more force required to make the cut, the less control you have. Because a sharp, properly shaped blade requires less force, it reduces fatigue, resulting in a more enjoyable carving experience. Many novice carvers get discouraged because they are carving with a dull knife or a blade that is not shaped properly.

Sharpening is a simple process. If you boil it down to the basics, sharpening consists of rubbing a piece of metal against an abrasive

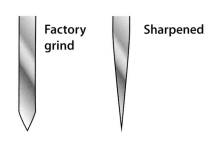

Factory grind   Sharpened

to create a wedge shape. For the abrasive, you can use anything from simple sandpaper to elaborate power sharpeners. You will start with a coarse abrasive to shape the blade, and then use progressively finer grits to remove the scratches until you have a polished edge.

There are many methods and products to help you achieve a

sharp cutting edge, but I recommend beginners start with sandpaper. Use spray adhesive to attach 6" (152mm)-long strips of sandpaper to a perfectly flat surface, such as glass or medium-density fiberboard (MDF). For the initial shaping, start with 200- to 320-grit wet/dry sandpaper, which is more durable than regular sandpaper. Work your way up through the grits to 600 grit, and then polish the blade on a leather strop.

Begin shaping the bevel. Hold the entire length of the blade flat against 200- or 320-grit sandpaper with the cutting edge facing away from you. Lift the back of the blade slightly (about ⅟₃₂", or 1mm). Maintain the same angle as you push the knife away from you, toward the cutting edge, and along the length of the sandpaper.

Shape the other side of the blade. Lift the blade off the sandpaper and flip the knife over so the cutting edge is facing toward you. Lay the entire length of the blade on the sandpaper and lift the back slightly (⅟₃₂", or 1mm). Pull the blade toward the cutting edge, along the length of the sandpaper, maintaining a consistent angle.

3

Finish shaping the bevel. Follow Steps 1 and 2 until you create the desired bevel across the length of the blade. You should see shiny metal where you've removed the old bevel and reshaped the blade.

4

Remove the scratches from the coarser sandpaper. Repeat Steps 1 through 3 using 400-grit and then 600-grit sandpaper. Remove the visible scratches from the coarser sandpaper before moving to the next finer grit.

✐ Keep a Pencil Handy

When you are starting a new project, lightly sketch it on the wood before you begin whittling. As you remove small slices and chips, some folks find it helpful to redraw the details that you have cut off. Some carvers and whittlers keep a small pencil on a string around their neck or connected through a buttonhole just for this purpose.

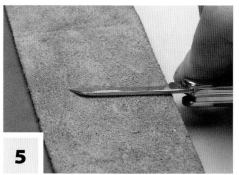

5

Polish the edge. Purchase a leather strop or glue a piece of leather, such as an old belt, to a flat piece of wood with the rough side facing up. Apply a small amount of stropping compound to the leather. (Stropping compound is available in powder form at hardware and auto parts stores. The grit is not important for stropping carving knives.) Position the entire length of the blade on the leather strop and lift the back of the blade slightly (1/32", or 1mm). Draw the blade across the strop, moving away from the cutting edge. Do not push the blade toward the cutting edge or you will damage the strop and round the cutting edge. At the end of the strop, lift the blade, flip the knife over, and place the other side flat on the strop. Lift the back of the blade slightly (1/32", or 1mm) and draw the blade along the strop, moving away from the cutting edge. This process polishes the blade for a cleaner and smoother cut.

Once you have shaped the bevel, you only need to sharpen with sandpaper if you nick the blade or damage the cutting edge. However, you must maintain the cutting edge by stropping often. When whittling for an extended period, you may have to strop the blade several times. You should be able to feel when the blade is getting a bit dull and in need of a touch-up strop. Form a habit of stropping the blade at the end of each whittling session.

A good way to tell if the knife blade is really sharp is to take a small piece of a dark wood, such as cedar or walnut, and make a long slicing cut across the end grain. If the blade is very sharp, the sliced surface should be shiny. If there are nearly invisible nicks on the blade, they will leave white streaks in the sliced surface.

Finishing

There are several ways to complete and finish your whittled pieces. After you have completed the basic whittling, you can sand the piece smooth or leave it as-is. In fact, you may want to try whittling the piece in such a manner that large flat areas are achieved and remain. This is called flat-plane carving and is quite popular. If you decide to stain or paint your piece, make sure to carve off all of the surfaces, as uncarved wood takes paint or stain differently than carved wood does.

You may need to scrub the carving to remove pencil marks, soil from handling, and/or clean up wood "fuzzies" at the bottoms of cuts. Use a denture brush, hot water, and dish detergent to scrub your project. If you scrub the piece, let it dry before applying any finish.

If you're interested in painting your projects, I suggest using thinned acrylic paints. Some whittlers and carvers like to use a woodburner to burn the line between each of the colors that

I use thinned acrylic paints to color my carvings.

will be painted. This woodburned line not only prevents the colors from wicking into each other, but also darkens the wood under the paint to create additional shadowing. If you decide to stain a carving, apply a wood conditioner or sealer first, and then the stain. Finally, apply a coat or two of polyurethane to protect the project. If you decide to leave the piece natural, you still may want to apply wood sealer and then a coat of polyurethane or wax.

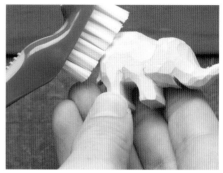

Use a denture brush, hot water, and dish detergent to remove any wood "fuzz," pencil marks, and dirt from your carving.

Index ————————————————————

Note: Page numbers in *italics* indicate projects.

About the Author

Tom Hindes, like many others carvers, discovered woodcarving during retirement. After a career in teaching industrial arts and technical training development, he rediscovered a fondness for working with wood. At first, this interest took the form of cabinet making, but after a few years, Tom wanted to work with something smaller and lighter. He began carving Noah's arks, complete with the pairs of animals, and immediately was hooked on carving.

After years of carving, he put his skills as a technical training developer into creating projects for beginning carvers. He decided to focus on whittling, or carving with one knife, as the medium for these projects. Whittling helped keep the projects easy, fast, and fun!

His first such project, "The 5-Minute Wizard," was published in *Woodcarving Illustrated* Summer 2008 (Issue 43) and was extremely popular. After that success, he contributed more articles to *Woodcarving Illustrated*, all of which focused on learning to whittle smaller, simplified projects like Santas, gnomes, wizards, and animals. It is his hope with both his articles and *20-Minute Whittling Projects* that beginners view the projects and say, "I can do that!"